NAVIGATING GROWTH FOR SMALL BUSINESSES

A Thorough, Step-by-Step Blueprint for Achieving Business Success

TOM GREENWOOD

TABLE OF CONTENT

INTRODUCTION

An entrepreneur by the name of Alex resided in the middle of the symphony of aspiration and opportunity, which was woven into the pattern of metropolitan landscapes that were humming with activity. His narrative was not simply a story about ambition; rather, it was a story about dogged determination, strategic planning, and the transformational power of knowledge.

The beginning of Alex's career as an entrepreneur began with an ardent vision, which served as a spark that kindled a drive to construct something that was significant. His early days were a frenzy of trial and error, and he had to navigate the maze of uncertainty. On the other hand, he discovered, amongst the mayhem, the unshakable significance of having a distinct vision, which serves as a compass that directs every choice and activity.

The foundation of his development was found to be strategic planning, which consisted of a blueprint that was weaved with SMART goals and stages that could be taken. As Alex's journey progresses, the need of market research becomes more apparent. Market research sheds light on the ways in which he may better grasp the requirements of his audience and decode the competitive environment.

In spite of the fact that Alex's growth was threatened by financial storms, he was able to harness the power of his financial expertise, which included a toolbox full of budgeting, forecasting, and cash flow management. These were more than simply instruments for survival; they became motors that propelled his aspirations closer and closer to becoming a reality.

He took his previously little startup and turned it into a powerhouse of efficiency via the application of operational finesse. Through the perspective of Alex's experiences, this book uncovers the intricacies of operational excellence, the hidden ingredient powering scalability and sustained success.

But beneath the spreadsheets and organizational acumen, Alex's narrative celebrates the core of entrepreneurship—the client. It's here that the pages of this book unfold into a tapestry of client experiences and relationship management tactics. Each connection became a building brick of trust, loyalty, and advocacy—a tribute to the power of outstanding service.

His crew, carefully picked to suit his abilities, matured into a cohesive entity driven by a shared mission. Together, they developed a culture of creativity and camaraderie—a backbone for sustainable success.

In the chronicles of Alex's journey and the revelations within these pages, this book materializes—a collection of techniques, ideas, and actionable knowledge. It's a blueprint for entrepreneurs navigating the rough waters of business growth—a manual exposing the skills to negotiate problems, capture opportunities, and create a legacy of entrepreneurial victory.

CHAPTER 1

Understanding Your Business Landscape

Understanding your company environment is similar to researching the terrain before starting on a difficult journey. The first chapter of the book "Navigating Growth for Small Businesses" acts as a compass, helping entrepreneurs through the critical stages of recognizing the sophisticated ecology in which their firms' function.

The Importance of Understanding

Growth is not a random attempt; rather, it is a planned and educated process. Entrepreneurs must first comprehend their existing situation before setting sail for growth. This entails a thorough evaluation—an introspective look at the company's strengths, flaws, opportunities, and dangers.

This reflection is about creating a deep understanding of the business's DNA, not only identifying triumphs or problems. It is about determining what distinguishes the company from rivals, understanding consumer wants and expectations, and knowing the market dynamics in which the company works.

Assessing the Playing Field

A SWOT analysis (Strengths, Weaknesses, Opportunities, and Threats) is a key tool for this process. It is not just a list of qualities, but rather a rigorous investigation of the internal and external elements impacting the firm. The internal landscape is illuminated by strengths and weaknesses, while the exterior world is illuminated by possibilities and dangers.

This chapter also highlights the need of setting clear objectives and developing a compelling vision. Goals operate as lighthouses, directing all decisions and actions toward a predetermined destination. They give the firm and its stakeholders with direction, focus, and incentive. A vision, on the other hand, is the North Star—a clear portrayal of what the company strives to be, motivating and uniting everyone in pursuit of a single goal.

Navigating the Difficulties

Understanding the corporate world is a process, not a static task. It entails continuing market research, paying close attention to client input, and closely monitoring industry changes. It is about being adaptable to changes, nimble enough to alter plans, and imaginative enough to capitalize on new possibilities.

Furthermore, this chapter calls for a comprehensive strategy. It is not enough to grasp figures or market trends; it is also necessary to empathize with the audience. It is about understanding the emotional connection that consumers desire, the issues that they want to address, and the experiences that they value.

Introduction to Small Business Growth.

The first chapter of "Navigating Growth for Small Businesses" acts as a light illuminating the importance of growth and its significant influence on small enterprises.

The Growth Imperative

Small companies are living creatures that thrive within changing environments, not static entities. Growth is not a choice; it is required for existence and success. This chapter stresses that growth is more than just growing sales or client base; it is also about evolution, resilience, and being relevant in a competitive marketplace.

Evolutionary

In the context of business, growth symbolizes evolution—a natural path toward reaching an enterprise's full potential. It personifies the spirit of flexibility, invention, and improvement. Small firms that welcome growth embrace change, accepting chances to enhance their services, optimize processes, and achieve new heights.

Competitor Resilience

Growth provides small companies with the resilience they need to face difficulties in an ever-changing industry. It's not just about surviving; it's about flourishing in the face of hardship. Businesses that actively seek development establish solid foundations, allowing them to weather storms, pivot as needed, and emerge stronger from setbacks.

The Effect on Stakeholders

Growth has an influence on more than just the firm; it also has an impact on workers, consumers, and the community. Increased expansion often translates into additional employment opportunities, better customer service, and a larger contribution to the local economy. It instills a feeling of pride and pleasure in individuals who work for the company.

Making a Journey Plan

This chapter establishes the tone for the book's journey, urging entrepreneurs to embrace development as a mentality, a strategic necessity, and a driver of good change. It stresses that progress is an intentional, well-informed undertaking anchored in defined objectives, careful techniques, and constant learning.

Assessment of Current

"Assessment of Current State" in "Navigating Growth for Small Businesses" reveals the critical process of introspection, in which entrepreneurs measure their business's position via a strategic SWOT analysis— examining strengths, weaknesses, opportunities, and threats.

Experiencing the Internal Terrain

Entrepreneurs start on this journey with the intuitive sense that knowing the present is critical to influencing the future. The SWOT analysis serves as a compass, directing them through an in-depth examination of their company's internal terrain.

Using Strengths to Address Weaknesses

Strengths emerge as the cornerstones around which success is based. This chapter emphasizes the necessity of identifying and using one's assets, whether they be a unique product, great service, or a brilliant personnel. Simultaneously, it necessitates the open admission of flaws. Identifying opportunities for improvement opens the door to strengthening the firm against threats.

Taking Advantage of Opportunities and Mitigating Threats

Beyond the sphere of internal causes, the external world contains both possibilities and risks. "Assessment of Current State" highlights the need of capitalizing on possibilities, whether they be growing markets, technology breakthroughs, or changing consumer habits. On the other hand, it cautions entrepreneurs to be wary of possible concerns such as rival moves, economic upheavals, or regulatory changes.

Making Strategic Decisions

This chapter serves as a starting point for making informed decisions. It argues for a more detailed view of the current state of the firm, directing entrepreneurs away from rash decisions and toward strategic steps aligned with recognized strengths and opportunities while reducing weaknesses and dangers.

Defining Goals and Vision

"Defining Goals and Vision" is a vital chapter in "Navigating Growth for Small Businesses," highlighting the critical significance of defined, realistic goals and a compelling vision in leading a firm toward success.

Goals: Progress Anchors

This chapter promotes the art of developing SMART objectives—specific, measurable, attainable, relevant, and time-bound goals. It explains the value of setting these milestones as guiding lights, driving every aspect of the company towards a certain goal. Whether it's sales objectives, market growth, or product innovation, goals give direction and purpose, encouraging a feeling of progress and achievement.

Making a Vision: Painting the Future

Among the solid framework of aims comes the ethereal but powerful force of vision. This chapter emphasizes the significance of a vivid and compelling vision—a light that illuminates the way ahead. A well-crafted vision is more than just financial goals; it captures the spirit of the company's mission, values, and intended effect on the world. It brings stakeholders together, motivates them, and acts as a guiding principle in decision-making.

Focus and alignment

"Defining Goals and Vision" promotes goal and vision alignment. It emphasizes the necessity of ensuring that each objective aligns with the larger vision, generating coherence and synergy within the corporate plan. This alignment fosters a feeling of concentration, reducing distraction and creating a determined effort toward a shared goal.

Accountability and Motivation

Goals and vision are not static notions; they are dynamic forces moving the company forward. This chapter highlights the need of frequent appraisal, adjustment, and celebration of milestones reached. It emphasizes the importance of these aspects in building a motivated workforce, promoting responsibility, and establishing a culture of continual development.

CHAPTER 2

Crafting a Robust Business Strategy

A solid business plan serves as the cornerstone for long-term success in small businesses. This chapter of the book discusses the critical function of a well-defined strategy in managing the intricacies of the corporate world.

A solid strategy starts with a detailed examination of market dynamics, consumer behavior, and competition positioning. Entrepreneurs get essential insights from rigorous market research, detecting trends, unmet requirements, and prospective possibilities.

These insights form the foundation of a compelling value proposition, a unique offering that differentiates a company in its market. This chapter promotes continual innovation, pushing firms to improve their goods or services in order to retain a competitive advantage. It promotes adaptability, enabling flexibility in response to changing market trends.

Furthermore, a solid company plan is not stagnant; it changes with the firm. Aligned with strategic objectives and vision, it stays nimble, incorporating real-time analytics to enable purposeful and informed choices, maintaining the business's forward momentum in an ever-changing context.

Market Research and Target Audience

Market research acts as a guidepost for organizations, navigating the complexity of customer behavior and market dynamics. It is more than just data collecting; it is a journey to discover the audience's motivations, wants, and goals.

Understanding the target audience is more than just knowing their demographics; it also entails empathizing with their objectives, obstacles, and emotional triggers that influence their choices. Creating thorough client profiles helps in the development of offers that strongly connect with them.

Market research provides priceless insights into developing trends, unmet demands, and unexplored possibilities. Businesses may modify their goods, develop services, and create effective marketing plans using this information.

These insights help companies to modify and enhance their strategy to meet market expectations. Whether it's modifying pricing, tweaking features, or redesigning marketing strategies, data-driven choices pave the road for long-term success.

Furthermore, market research is a continuous interaction with clients rather than a one-time effort. Listening carefully and reacting to their input helps to establish connections and demonstrate a customer-centric attitude.

Market research and knowing the target audience, in essence, constitute the foundation of informed decision-making and customer-centricity. Businesses not only achieve success but also develop long-term relationships with their customers by comprehending market complexities and empathizing with their audience.

Value Proposition

A value proposition, at its core, encompasses the distinct advantage or solution that a company provides to its clients. It extends beyond goods or services, addressing unique client demands or pain areas in a way that distinguishes the company from rivals.

Understanding the demands of the consumer is critical. Thorough market research and sympathetic analysis assist firms in learning what genuinely matters to their target customer. This knowledge serves as the foundation for developing a compelling value offer.

A compelling value offer is not only about being different; it is also about being noticeably superior. It underlines the reasons why a client should pick one company over another. This distinctiveness might be due to distinguishing characteristics, higher quality, great service, or new solutions.

In a value proposition, clarity and simplicity are essential. It must be succinct, understandable, and engaging enough to catch attention quickly. A well-articulated value proposition highlights the primary advantage that a consumer obtains by doing business with the company.

It is critical to focus on the advantages for consumers. A strong value proposition focuses on how the product or service solves issues, satisfies wants, or improves people's lives. Highlighting these advantages helps to establish a closer connection with the audience.

Developing a successful value proposition often requires testing and iteration. Experimenting with several versions, obtaining feedback, and revising the proposal based on insights are all critical. It's a fluid process that changes as the company learns more about its target audience and market.

It is critical to smoothly integrate the value proposition into marketing initiatives. It forms the backbone of communications across several channels—website, commercials, sales presentations, and so forth. Consistent and unambiguous communication enhances the value provided, making it more appealing to prospective clients.

The value proposition is a promise rather than a statement. It represents the distinct value that a company provides to its clients, altering their views and influencing their choices. Businesses that provide a compelling value offer not only attract clients but also lay the groundwork for long-term connections and sustainable success.

Business Model Innovation

Business Model Innovation stands as a revolutionary technique within the development story of small firms, explained in "Navigating Growth for Small Businesses." It's a dynamic strategy that transcends established conventions, seeking creative options for income generating, collaborations, and distribution outlets.

A business model innovation is about reinventing how a firm develops, delivers, and collects value. It disrupts standard norms, urging entrepreneurs to seek new viewpoints, accept change, and explore unknown territory within their industry.

One component of this innovation resides in income creation. It forces organizations to rethink their present income streams while exploring and experimenting with new options. This might include broadening product offerings, creating subscription models, or merging complementary services to provide other income channels.

Moreover, business model innovation relies on building strategic collaborations. It's about cooperating with complementary firms or organizations to develop synergies that magnify value. Whether it's via joint ventures, strategic alliances, or co-branding projects, these collaborations can provide access to new markets, resources, and expertise that drive development.

Distribution channels play a vital part in this innovation as well. It's about analyzing current distribution strategies and discovering new paths to reach clients efficiently. Embracing digital platforms, direct-to-consumer tactics, or using new technology for distribution may transform a business's reach and accessibility.

This innovation isn't only about drastic breakthroughs; it's also about modest gains. It includes ongoing experimentation and refining in business processes, customer experiences, and operational efficiency. Iterating on current models while investigating innovative techniques develops adaptation and resilience.

Successful business model innovation needs a mentality shift—an openness to welcome uncertainty and a willingness to question the current quo. It thrives on a culture of innovation, where ideas are fostered, tested, and polished. Businesses that promote an atmosphere favorable to innovation typically find themselves at the forefront of industry revolution.

Moreover, timing is key. Businesses need to determine ideal opportunities to adopt changes, considering industry trends, client wants, and technical improvements. Being proactive rather than reactive to market fluctuations helps organizations to remain ahead in a continually dynamic field.

Ultimately, business model innovation is a strategic facilitator of success, giving firms with the agility and flexibility to succeed in changing marketplaces. It's a continual journey—a dedication to researching, adapting, and reinventing company strategies to generate sustainable value, promote resilience, and capture new possibilities.

CHAPTER 3

Building a Strong Foundation

Building a solid foundation for a small company serves as the cornerstone of sustained development and success. This foundation comprises several facets, from operational efficiency and financial management to team development and leadership.

Operational efficiency constitutes the core of a robust corporate foundation. It includes simplifying procedures, workflows, and operations to enhance efficiency and decrease waste. Assessing and refining these internal systems not only boosts efficiency but also cultivates a culture of constant improvement. Businesses that emphasize operational excellence find themselves better positioned to respond to changing market circumstances and grow effectively.

Financial management is another key aspect. It entails smart budgeting, controlling cash flow, and making financial predictions. Sound financial processes not only assure stability but also assist strategic decision-making. By having a comprehensive picture of the financial health of the firm, entrepreneurs can manage resources efficiently, reduce risks, and capitalize on growth possibilities.

Team development and leadership are key parts of constructing a solid foundation. Hiring the proper individuals, developing a great work culture, and cultivating effective leadership are crucial. A cohesive and motivated team aligned with the business's goal contributes greatly to its success. Strong leadership stimulates creativity, fosters cooperation, and creates an atmosphere favorable to development.

Furthermore, technology plays a key part in current business foundations. Embracing technology improvements simplifies processes, boosts communication, and gives important insights via data analytics. Integrating technology into company operations frequently leads to enhanced efficiency and competitiveness.

Legal and regulatory compliance is a crucial but frequently ignored component of a firm foundation. Ensuring compliance with relevant rules and regulations defends the firm against possible risks and liabilities. It creates a stable climate for development, safeguarding both the firm and its stakeholders.

Moreover, creating excellent connections with suppliers, partners, and consumers helps considerably to the foundation. Cultivating these connections promotes trust, dependability, and loyalty, creating the framework for long-term success and progress.

Successful entrepreneurs recognize that constructing a solid foundation is not a one-time activity but a continuing commitment. It demands adaptation, resilience, and a desire to change. As the business environment develops, so must the foundation upon which the firm stands. Continuous review, adaptation, and development are vital to keeping a solid foundation despite shifting market conditions.

Operational efficiency isn't just a phrase; it's the art of doing things better, not harder. It's the painstaking study of how every wheel spins inside a firm, searching out inefficiencies and converting them into chances for progress. From the way things are stored to how consumer queries are addressed, no stone is left unturned.

This search for efficiency manifests in numerous ways. Firstly, it's about deconstructing complicated processes, dissecting them to their essence, and recreating them to run flawlessly. The goal? To reduce redundancy and simplify paths, ensuring that every operation leads to maximum production with little waste.

Accompanying this process improvement is the orchestration of workflows—a visual blueprint that directs jobs from idea to completion. Imagine a smoothly running river, unencumbered by superfluous obstructions. That's the goal—a system where work proceeds seamlessly, reducing delays and mistakes along the route.

Technology has a leading role in this story. It's the unsung hero that automates everyday activities, reduces difficulties, and helps enterprises to work at lightning speed. Imagine leveraging technologies that revolutionize how data is managed, projects are done, and customer contacts are handled—effectiveness heightened by digital prowess.

Yet, efficiency isn't only about procedures and equipment; it's a cultural approach. It flourishes in an atmosphere that fosters creativity, where every team member is encouraged to submit ideas for development. It's about building a culture where efficiency becomes an intrinsic element of how things are done.

Moreover, this desire for efficiency isn't static; it's forward-thinking. It's about planning for growth—building systems and processes that stretch and extend without breaking under strain. Think of it as developing a sturdy framework, one that evolves smoothly as the firm thrives.

Continuous assessment is the compass that guides this trip. Metrics and KPIs function as lighthouses, revealing opportunities for improvement. It's not about perfection but about continual evolution—a dedication to refining and upgrading operations to satisfy the ever-changing needs of the market.

Financial Management

Financial management constitutes the foundations upon which the architecture of a profitable company stands—a sub-chapter covered thoroughly within the wisdom of "Navigating Growth for Small Businesses." Imagine this section as a treasure map leading to the financial success and sustainability of a firm. It uncovers the strategic relevance of generating and controlling budgets, cash flow, and financial projections, each acting as a critical foundation sustaining continuous development.

Picture the formulation of a budget not simply as figures on a ledger, but as a strategic painting that paints the financial environment of a corporation. It's a painstaking procedure, analogous to developing a precise plan, calculating the route of resources, and distributing them prudently. A well-structured budget isn't only a plan; it's a financial blueprint directing choices, ensuring resources are funneled efficiently toward defined goals.

Enter the arena of cash flow management—a delicate orchestration ensuring the lifeblood of the firm stays constant and throbbing. It's analogous to directing a symphony, managing the influx and outflow of funds. This sub-chapter uncovers the necessity of monitoring this flow with accuracy, forecasting undulations, and maintaining a strong balance between income and costs. After all, a well-maintained cash flow isn't just about surviving; it's about prospering amongst the unpredictable currents of the economic world.

Consider financial predictions as the compass leading the firm through new terrain. They're not crystal balls but calculative views into the future—insights generated from existing patterns and forecasts. It calls for the establishment of these projections, helping firms to manage probable pitfalls and embrace exciting possibilities, all within the tapestry of calibrated risk.

Peering deeper, financial management isn't just about balancing accounts; it's about controlling risks and planning for eventualities. It's comparable to reinforcing the castle against prospective threats—be it economic changes or unanticipated bills. Understanding and minimizing these risks via good planning and preparation improves resilience in the face of unpredictability.

Amidst figures and ledgers lies the skill of strategic decision-making. The art of financial management provides a picture of financial insights directing the helm of the ship. It's about applying these insights to direct the course—whether forging new initiatives, growing operations, or maximizing resources. Financial planning becomes the guiding light illuminating the route to progress and wealth.

In today's digital world, technology plays a key role. It's the wind in the sails, driving financial management ahead. Imagine state-of-the-art technologies as the ship's engines— automating operations, evaluating data fast, and allowing real-time decision-making. Embracing technology isn't simply an option; it's a must for companies to flourish in an ever-evolving financial world.

Team Building and Leadership

Team building and leadership are the cornerstone factors required for developing a cohesive and flourishing working environment inside any small company landscape. Beyond simple organizational jargon, they embody the essence of unity, synergy, and direction needed for attaining group objectives and accelerating progress.

Team building is the practice of cultivating connections and establishing a feeling of camaraderie among workers inside a business. It exceeds standard ice-breaking exercises; it's about building an environment where every team member feels appreciated, understood, and part of something greater. It's developing trust, enabling open communication, and fostering a collaborative atmosphere.

Effective team building sparks the synergy of varied abilities, stimulating creativity, innovation, and problem-solving. By breaking down barriers and developing bridges between team members, it converts a collection of people into a cohesive unit working towards a common goal. It cultivates a culture where diversity are valued, viewpoints are respected, and collaborative successes are appreciated.

Leadership serves as the guiding force driving the ship of a corporation toward success. It's not only about having a position; it's about motivating, encouraging, and helping people to attain their full potential. Effective leadership produces an atmosphere where people are driven, encouraged to develop, and empowered to take responsibility of their tasks.

Great leaders lead by example, embracing the ideals they espouse. They offer a compelling vision, unifying everyone around similar goals. They listen intently, giving direction and support while building an atmosphere that stimulates learning and personal growth.

Leadership isn't restricted to a single figure; it's a trait that penetrates across an organization. It may arise from any level, cultivating a culture where leadership traits—such as responsibility, empathy, and resilience—are nurtured and recognized.

When team building and leadership converge, they produce a symbiotic connection that generates success. Effective leaders realize the relevance of a cohesive team and actively cultivate an atmosphere where team development thrives. Conversely, successful teams strengthen and support the vision of their leaders, fostering development and innovation.

This synergy generates an environment where trust, respect, and cooperation flourish. It's a dynamic where leaders empower their teams, and teams, in turn, elevate their leaders through devotion, loyalty, and commitment to shared objectives.

CHAPTER 4

Marketing and Branding Strategies

Marketing and branding strategies act as the compass directing organizations towards recognition and development. They cover approaches and tactics used to sell items or services while developing a distinctive personality. These techniques affect how consumers perceive and engage with a brand, building loyalty and boosting market reach. Effective marketing and branding activities not only separate a firm from rivals but also generate lasting impressions, persuading consumers to interact and identify with the brand's values and products.

Effective Branding

Effective branding in the enormous world of business is more than simply a logo or a snappy phrase; it is the art of storytelling that captivates hearts and minds. It's about creating a story that goes beyond just goods or services and connects with consumers on a deeper level.

A captivating brand narrative starts with authenticity—the true core of what the company represents. It's about revealing the brand's fundamental values, purpose, and the one-of-a-kind journey that defines its existence. An real narrative, whether it's one of resilience, invention, or a desire to change, serves as the cornerstone for a brand's identity.

Furthermore, great branding is more than simply conveying a narrative; it is about generating emotions. It's all about forging a tie between the brand and its audience. Emotions last longer than facts or data; they are the glue that holds a brand in the hearts and minds of its customers. A brand that emotionally connects with a customer becomes a part of their narrative.

Visual storytelling—a symphony of colors, typography, and images that communicates volumes—is required to create an engaging brand image. It is about developing a visual language that expresses the brand's personality and values without the need of words. The correct visual components elicit emotions, establish moods, and leave a lasting impression.

Effective branding is built on consistency. It is consistency in message, aesthetics, and experience across all touchpoints. Consistency fosters trust and strengthens the brand's identity. Every encounter, whether via the website, social media, packaging, or customer service, develops the brand narrative.

Understanding your audience is critical. Effective branding resonates when it appeals directly to the target audience's wants, needs, and goals. It's about understanding their preferences, difficulties, and speaking their language. Brands that recognize and address their target audience's pain points become partners in their journey.

Flexibility and flexibility are also important considerations. Consumer tastes and market environments change as the globe changes. Effective branding is dynamic, able to evolve while remaining faithful to its essential ideals. It changes with the times without losing its core.

Effective branding is really a symphony of authenticity, emotions, graphics, consistency, audience comprehension, and flexibility. It's a story that resonates, a picture that captivates, and an experience that customers will remember.

When done correctly, good branding becomes a lighthouse, directing people to a brand they trust and identify with.

Digital Presence

In today's company world, having a strong digital presence isn't a choice; it's a must. It is about utilizing the power of digital platforms to expand a brand's reach, create interaction, and develop meaningful connections with the audience.

Digital presence is a multidimensional strategy that incorporates many digital marketing methods. At its heart is the world of digital marketing—a diverse toolkit that includes SEO, content marketing, email campaigns, and pay-per-click advertising. It is all about improving online exposure, ensuring that a brand shows prominently when customers search for connected items or services.

Social media platforms have become critical in defining a brand's online identity. They're more than just places to share information; they're interactive areas where companies can communicate with their customers in real time. It's about telling interesting stories, delivering relevant material, and connecting with followers honestly. Social media encourages debate and builds a community around a business.

A great digital presence goes beyond marketing to provide an outstanding online experience. This includes user-friendly webpages, intuitive interfaces, and smooth navigation. It is about optimizing for mobile devices and ensuring that every encounter creates a favorable image, resulting in increased user engagement and satisfaction.

Furthermore, exploiting internet platforms works hand in hand with data analytics. It is all about evaluating data insights to constantly improve strategy. Analyzing user activity, measuring data, and knowing audience preferences enable firms to adjust their digital presence, ensuring it closely fits with audience expectations.

E-commerce has transformed how firms operate in the digital arena. E-commerce tactics that permit frictionless transactions are part of a good digital presence. It is about establishing an online purchasing experience that is easy, safe, and convenient, hence increasing consumer happiness and loyalty.

Building a strong digital presence entails more than simply being there; it also entails being remembered. It is about leaving an online imprint that people remember. A strong digital presence, when implemented properly, promotes trust, credibility, and loyalty. It establishes a brand as an authority figure in its sector, increasing its exposure and impact in the digital sphere.

Customer Relationship Management

Customer Relationship Management (CRM) serves as the cornerstone of sustainable corporate success, concentrating on techniques that transcend basic transactions to build enduring ties with customers. It's a strategy that centers around understanding, engaging, and cultivating connections to generate devoted advocates for a company.

At its foundation, good CRM starts with knowing clients beyond their purchase behaviors. It requires diving into their wants, preferences, and pain spots. By utilizing data analytics and consumer input, organizations obtain important insights that allow customized interactions and bespoke experiences.

Communication is the core of CRM tactics. It s about keeping an open communication via numercus touchpoints—be it email, social media, or in-person contact. Timely and relevant communication, whether it's offering product updates, requesting feedback, or expressing thanks, deepens the link between a company and its consumers.

Building trust is crucial in CRM. Transparency, dependability, and consistency in fulfilling commitments cement trust. Brands that stress openness in their transactions and display consistency in their offerings develop a foundation of credibility, building durable partnerships built on mutual trust.

CRM isn't only about acquisition; it extends to post-purchase interaction. Effective post-sale assistance, prompt customer care, and tailored follow-ups indicate a brand's commitment beyond the moment of sale. Addressing complaints swiftly and delivering answers encourage long-term loyalty.

Personalization is a crucial driver in current CRM tactics. Tailoring experiences based on individual tastes and behaviors helps clients feel appreciated. Whether it's proposing bespoke items or delivering special deals, customization enriches the consumer experience, establishing deeper relationships.

Furthermore, CRM involves consumer feedback and active listening. Gathering feedback assists in determining consumer satisfaction levels and areas for development. It's important not only listening but also acting on criticism, proving to clients that their ideas count.

Moreover, loyalty programs and consumer awards play a key part in CRM. Offering incentives for repeat purchases or loyalty benefits cultivates a feeling of belonging and gratitude, encouraging consumers to remain involved with the company.

CHAPTER 5

Scaling and Expansion

Scaling and growth are crucial milestones in the path of every successful firm. This chapter is a compass navigating the transforming process of development, transcending simply survival to embrace new vistas of potential. Scaling isn't just about growing operations; it's a strategic development that involves careful planning, creativity, and adaptation.

At its heart, scaling requires raising a company model to meet rising demands while retaining efficiency and quality. It's about setting a road towards growth without sacrificing the basic principles or losing sight of the original aim. This chapter digs into the subtleties of scaling—a path defined by obstacles, victories, and strategic choices that move an organization towards sustainable development. It's an investigation of methodology, best practices, and insights crucial for organizations seeking to extend their horizons and prosper in an ever-evolving market context.

Scalability and Adaptability

Scalability and flexibility are critical groundwork in the complex world of corporate development, steering organizations through the ever-changing tides of market dynamics. Scalability is more than just expansion; it is the skill of laying a base that can expand without sacrificing efficiency or quality.

Scalable processes need rigorous planning to ensure that systems, operations, and infrastructure can handle rising demand. It is about creating agile frameworks that can bend and change as the company expands, while maintaining a balance of growth and stability.

Adaptability, on the other hand, refers to a company's ability to adapt in the face of change. Consumer preferences, technical improvements, and economic volatility all affect market dynamics. Being flexible implies being able to quickly pivot, innovate, and readjust methods in order to successfully navigate through these changes.

Businesses that place a premium on scalability invest in technology and procedures that can readily adapt to rising workloads or market demands. It is about automating tedious work, optimizing operations, and cultivating an innovative culture. Scalability guarantees that the company develops without sacrificing quality or client happiness.

Scalability is complemented with adaptability, which recognizes that change is unavoidable. To remain ahead, you must have contingency plans, diversify your services, and constantly evaluate market trends. A flexible company is agile, responsive, and willing to embrace new possibilities or change strategy as required.

Scalability and flexibility together generate a dynamic synergy inside a firm. Scalability offers the framework for expansion, while adaptability adds agility and resilience. It's a balancing act between scaling and adapting without sacrificing stability.

Scalability and flexibility are not independent notions in successful firms, but rather interwoven tactics. They create an atmosphere that fosters creativity, celebrates adaptability, and instills a mentality that views change as a chance for progress. Those that understand the delicate dance between scalability and flexibility not only survive but flourish in an ever-changing business environment, pushing their organizations to long-term success.

Partnerships and Collaboration

Partnerships and collaborations are powerful accelerators for corporate success, opening up new channels and synergies that catapult businesses to higher heights. These alliances are strategic ties that generate reciprocal advantages and common success in the complicated web of the commercial world, not merely shared objectives.

Exploring cooperation entails discovering complimentary abilities and common goals. It is about looking for collaborations that address gaps, broaden market reach, or provide creative solutions. Collaborations, whether a joint venture, a supplier relationship, or a strategic alliance with industry peers, use different knowledge and resources for mutual benefit.

Strategic alliances are founded on common values and visions. They are more than just contracts; they are relationships built on trust, mutual respect, and a shared commitment to success. Businesses form strategic partnerships to overcome obstacles, profit on opportunities, and accomplish collective objectives that exceed individual capabilities.

Effective communication and a cooperative attitude are essential for successful partnerships. The foundation of productive relationships is clear demarcation of tasks, agreed objectives, and open communication channels. Collaboration entails not just sharing resources but also information, ideas, and experiences that benefit all parties involved.

Strategic alliances also promote innovation and drive development. They provide you access to new markets, technology, or distribution methods, giving you more room to grow. Collaboration allows firms to tap into untapped potentials, encourage innovation, and open doors to new possibilities.

Partnerships generate development and sustainability in today's linked corporate world. They increase strengths, compensate for flaws, and boost competitiveness. Businesses may grow operations, minimize risks, and enter new markets more effectively by using cooperation.

Furthermore, partnerships are not limited to external collaborations; cultivating an internal collaborative culture inside a business is also important. Encourage cross-departmental collaboration, teamwork, and information exchange to improve efficiency, creativity, and overall organizational development.

Partnerships and collaborations, in essence, exemplify the phrase "strength in unity." They enable organizations to collaborate across borders, combine resources, and embark on journeys toward mutual prosperity. Businesses handle the challenges of the market environment by using the combined power of collaborations and strategic partnerships, consolidating their position and achieving sustainable development.

International Expansion

International company expansion is a critical but complex activity that brings a plethora of possibilities and problems. Entering global markets requires a thorough awareness of various cultures, markets, rules, and customer habits.

Assessing foreign growth potential starts with market research and analysis. It entails finding target markets that are compatible with the company's services and growth goals. Evaluating market demand, competitiveness, economic stability, and cultural subtleties aids in evaluating realistic growth opportunities.

Entering global marketplaces opens you a plethora of options. It enables organizations to reach new client groups, enter previously unexplored areas, and benefit from economies of scale. International growth promotes diversification by minimizing reliance on individual markets and lowering risks associated with volatility in local markets.

However, with opportunity come a slew of new obstacles. Adapting to different cultural standards, language constraints, and various customer habits may be difficult. Furthermore, managing complicated regulatory environments, legal systems, and geopolitical uncertainty requires careful planning and strategic thinking.

Maintaining consistency while respecting local tastes is one of the most difficult issues in international growth. To appeal with varied audiences without compromising the brand identity, it is necessary to balance uniform operations with specialized methods.

Logistical problems, such as supply chain complexity and infrastructure variations, are also hindrances. Effective logistics management is becoming more important in global marketplaces to guarantee smooth operations and on-time delivery.

Mitigating risks in foreign growth requires careful planning, extensive market research, and a strong risk management approach. Developing strategic alliances, localizing marketing strategies, and getting professional advice on legal and regulatory compliance are all critical stages in managing these hurdles.

Furthermore, technical improvements and digitization are critical in breaking down obstacles to worldwide growth. Utilizing technology improves communication, simplifies processes, and allows firms to reach a larger global audience more effectively.

A well-defined plan, flexibility, and agility are required for successful international growth. It requires a thorough awareness of global markets, a flexible strategy, and an unshakable commitment to addressing the different demands of global customers.

CONCLUSION

Throughout this book, we've begun on a trip across the complicated landscape of business growth and development, exploring a plethora of tactics and ideas crucial for nurturing and expanding organizations. Each chapter functioned as a compass, leading us through the intricacies and subtleties of developing a successful company, one step at a time.

We've dug into core topics including analyzing the company environment, evaluating the present situation, and creating clear objectives and ambitions. These chapters established the framework, highlighting the significance of introspection, strategic planning, and picturing the trajectory of progress.

Moreover, we've addressed the critical function of market research, designing appealing value propositions, and establishing effective company strategies. These chapters addressed the necessity of identifying your audience, creating distinctive value, and navigating the competitive environment with creativity and clarity.

Our trip spanned across crucial dimensions including operational efficiency, financial management, and team development, exposing the value of simplified operations, budgetary restraint, and cultivating a collaborative and motivated staff.

We've underlined the vital function of digital presence, customer relationship management, and branding tactics. These chapters underlined the necessity of adaptation, communication, and creating durable ties with clients in the digital world.

Additionally, we delved into the realms of scalability, flexibility, collaborations, and international growth, realizing the complexity, possibilities, and problems inherent in these strategic efforts.

The conclusion of these chapters isn't simply a collection of business concepts; it's a roadmap—a complete guide developed to inspire entrepreneurs and company executives. It's an invitation to continue the path of progress, equipped with information, insights, and a stronger determination to traverse the ever-evolving corporate market.

As you, the reader, go ahead, remember that development is a constant process—a continuous cycle of learning, adapting, and inventing. Embrace change as an opportunity, because inside change lay the seeds of development and evolution.

Remain nimble, sensitive to market fluctuations, and steadfast in your dedication to quality. Foster a culture of cooperation, creativity, and customer-centricity inside your firm. Seek collaborations that magnify strengths and seek new opportunities for advancement.

Leverage technology, exploit data-driven insights, and embrace digital transformation as a driver for success. Embody the qualities of honesty, integrity, and resilience in every area of your business journey.

Above all, remember that the core of your company is in the connections you nurture—with your staff, your customers, and your partners. Cherish these connections, because they are the pillars that maintain development and propel success.

As you read the last pages of this book, visualize the future of your firm with hope and commitment. Your adventure doesn't stop here; it's a precursor to the endless opportunities awaiting your entrepreneurial spirit. Embrace the obstacles, grasp the chances, and continue to develop, prosper, and make an unforgettable impact on the world of business.

MIKE ROSE

So You Want to Be a Social Media Manager

5 Secrets To Successful and Effective Social Media Management

Contents

Introduction

In this book, you'll find some of the most important lessons I had to learn the hard way through my last 10 years working in a marketing agency. During this time I wrote copy and designed social marketing campaigns for Fortune 50 companies, which I guarantee you've heard of though I'll be omitting their names (legal teams are scary.) You can say the information you'll learn from this book is the cheat codes for effective Social marketing and it will serve as the foundation for starting your career as a Social Media Manager.

Even if you fancy yourself as a creative writer, or if you're just dipping your toes into the social space, these lessons will help set you up for success and will change the way you approach Social marketing from the ground up.

Social Marketing is important for any business, and if you're not using it then you are missing out on an accessible way to massively scale your business. If you're the type who loathes the idea of TikTok dances, and Instagram selfies, keep in mind that's not what we'll be talking about here. Every brand-new smartphone comes pre-installed with at least one social media platform, which means I can say with absolute certainty that there is a touch point with your target audience on Social Media.

Every business needs marketing. Period. You could have the best product, or provide the best service, but if you're not marketing it to the public then it will be doomed to fail. You may be thinking to yourself "Well business thrived before Facebook even existed so why should I start now?" Well, the answer is businesses thrived in a pre-digital revolutionary age, and this book will help guide you into your digital renaissance.

Still not sold? Let's talk brass tax. Social advertising is far cheaper and more optimized than traditional marketing strategies, and even with as little as $100 a month, you can get more foot traffic, sales, or leads than you had in the last year. There are countless success stories of mom-and-pop restaurants, small-to-medium businesses, and single-person entrepreneurs who have found unbelievable success by leveraging simple and inexpensive Social marketing tactics. This can be you! Keep reading and I'll show you how.

If you are just starting your career or have decided to switch job titles and dive into social marketing then these tactics are for you. They have been tried and tested through 10 years of agency experience. 10 years of success and failure and taught me how to find scaled success from shoestring budgets to multimillion-dollar ones. Am I beating a dead horse? Yes, but I can't reiterate enough how valuable these lessons are for achieving success. There's value in learning from my mistakes, and this book is here to help you avoid them.

Chapter 1: Know Thy Target

Before we get into any fun tips and tricks, let's lay a foundation. Before you even bring a pen to paper or think about how you're going to begin marketing your product, you need to understand WHO YOUR TARGET AUDIENCE IS. Let that sink in. WHO YOUR TARGET AUDIENCE IS. The biggest mistake that marketers make is that they cast their targeting net far too wide and as a result, they miss out on the hungrier fish. Knowledge may be half the battle, but when it comes to social marketing it's nearly 80% of it.

Let's use an example of a mom-and-pop restaurant that has the best meatballs in town. We'll call them Rose's Pasta. Everyone likes to eat, so you may think your audience is Men and women aged 1 - 99 because everyone likes food, and you want as many people to come in for a meal. This would be a mistake. People love to eat, but think about your position in the market, and ultimately the kind of clientele you'd like to serve. Is Rose's Pasta a family restaurant? Or is it a swanky date spot? These are the types of questions you need to focus on to help narrow down that target. This will help guide you on the type of language or imagery you will want to lean into when building your campaigns. For example, If you're a family restaurant you may want to lean into the affordability of your meatballs and target people with kids, Men and women aged 30-55, in a 5-10 mile radius from your restaurant. This information gives you a much different image of the type of person you're trying to sell to. What kind of information do families care about? Affordability? A family-friendly atmosphere? Drink specials?

On the other hand, if you're business is a swanky date spot, your target will likely be much younger, and target an audience willing to pay more for the atmosphere. In this case, it's much more likely your target audience is Men and Women 21 - 40, single, and interested in happy hour specials and the potential to share your business atmosphere on their Instagram stories.

So why is this important? Both target audiences in this example are similar enough, why wouldn't you just cast the wide net to target both? The answer is that Social marketing gives you the option to target these specific demographic traits, and this will be the secret sauce to optimizing your social campaigns. Your budgets are limited regardless of how bloated they may be, so being effective with even the smallest amount of ad spend will help you get the most bang for your ad dollar. If we were positioned as the date spot, and targeted the wider audience, that means ads will be served to families who may be on tighter budgets and can not afford a $15 cocktail. This means you have wasted your marketing budget on an ad placement that does nothing for your business!

So take some time, put down this book, and identify who your target audience is. Be honest with the positioning of your product or service, and who you believe is the most likely to buy it. Keep in mind you don't need a 10-page dossier on their habits likes and life experiences.

A helpful exercise is creating a customer persona that helps shape and identify who your audiences may look like. Keep the following key demographic points top of mind: age, gender, life experience work role, marital status, hobbies, and geographic locations. Give them a name, and a personality, and breathe life into your customer persona. For example: For Rose's Pasta, the swanky date spot, we have

- David aged 32, is a tech professional living in Chicago and is single and ready to mingle. He loves Italian food, craft cocktails and has a passion for photography. He's never been big on brunch but will go crazy for a bottomless mimosa deal, and he is always looking for the best happy hour specials in town.

Keep it short and simple. Your created persona will help serve as a north star as you think about what and how you are going to sell your brand or service.

Chapter 2: Soul of Wit

So you created your target audience persona. Congrats that's 80% of the battle! Now let's get into some tips on how to construct what your messaging should say.

Keep it simple, stupid. Your messaging needs to be quick and punchy. If you can't get your message across in a few words, then reevaluate your message. The average attention span of a social reader is about ~3 seconds, so if you are writing a novel to sell business propositions then you're wasting your effort. Know what you want to say and say it clearly and directly.

You're probably wondering, "Well that's great, but how do I write things more concisely?" The biggest pitfall I've seen from those early in their careers is that they try to include every value proposition, every benefit, and every selling point in their social copy. This is a mistake. Effective copy sells a single digestible idea quickly. For example, let's say you're an at-home maid service named Rose's Maid Services, and your value propositions are that you are cheaper, more effective at cleaning homes thanks to a perfected maid training program, you use purely organic products and offer a unique dog poo pick up service in addition to house cleaning. On top of that you are also running a special this month for 50% off your next cleaning. All of these things set you apart from competitors, but speaking to all of them in a single post spreads your focus far too thin. You'd want to speak to each of these benefits individually to help keep your audience focused on the key ideas you want them to focus on. Social marketing gives you the ability to create multiple ads, and multiple iterations of the same post with different messaging to highlight exactly what you're trying to drive home.

So to optimize Rose's Cleaning Service's social campaign we'll want to break out each value proposition as its own selling point independent of one another. This will keep your messaging clear and direct. It's easier for your audience to digest that your service is cheaper than its competitors, or that you are running a special for your services than for them to remember every possible reason why they should choose your brand over your competitors. Less is almost always more when it comes to social copy.

But what should you write? Your target audience will largely dictate the tone, word choice, and direction of your social copy. Rose's Skateboards will want to use more casual diction vs Rose's luxury watches. Regardless of your brand's positioning remember your audience, and that your word choice matters in how your audience will perceive you. Do you want your audience to view you as fun? As the economical choice? As the silver bullet solution? Whatever your position, always keep in mind how the audience will perceive the words you use.

So how are we going to market Rose's Pasta: The Swanky Date Spot? We'll start by remembering David, our customer persona from Chapter One, and the different offerings we'd like to focus on that make us unique. In this case, we'll focus on the food menu, drink specials, and overall atmosphere of the restaurant. For example:

Variant 1:

- **Copy:** *Pasta is better when it's made for two. Reserve a table at Rose's Pasta for your next date night.*
- **Creative:** Spaghetti being shared by a couple, Lady and the Tramp style.

Variant 2:

- **Copy:** *Is it Happy Hour yet? Check out our latest drink specials every Monday through Friday from 3 - 6 pm. Make a reservation today!*
- **Creative:** A dynamic shot of a bartender mixing a drink.

Variant 3:

- **Copy:** *First impressions count. Make date night special at Rose's Pasta. Reserve a table now.*
- **Creative:** A photo of a dressed couple sharing a laugh on a first date.

Each of these variants serves a different purpose and highlights a different part of the business. This will also allow you to understand exactly what your audience truly cares about through data analytics, and we'll cover campaign analysis in a later chapter.

Another thing you may have noticed is across all three post variants, I've included a call to action (CTA). When publishing on Social we are ultimately trying to drive action from our audience. In this case, it's trying to drive them to make a reservation. Call-to-actions play a bit of a psychological game and help motivate people to do the action in the moment. That's why most TV infomercials end their videos with "Call now!" or "Buy today!" Always include a brief call to action that helps push audiences to take the desired reaction in ALL social posts. Not including a CTA is a dire mistake, and can be the difference between a successful and failed campaign.

So to recap your Social copy should be short and to the point. It should keep your audience top of mind, and it should include a call to action. Keep it simple, less is more, and motivate people to do the thing

Chapter 3: Tell a Story

Let's talk about traditional marketing for a second, specifically commercials during the Super Bowl where brands ranging from cars to candy bars spend millions of dollars on a 30-second television ad that millions of Americans watch. Take a moment and think about your favorite one. None of them have a talking head that tells you why you should buy their product over another, instead, they tell a story or try to pluck your heartstrings to invoke an emotion. This is what you should aim for in all forms of marketing, including on Social.

In a social context, this is typically done with imagery. Social copy can be brilliant but with the wrong image, it could fall flat. This is why you have to use both the copy and creative in tandem. If your image doesn't invoke the same message as your copy then you will be telling a conflicting story. The copy is the vocals, and the image is the beat and melody. You must be in concert with one another.

Let's look at Rose's Pasta: Swanky Date Spot once more. Let's say you're trying to highlight your drink specials, as you head into Valentine's Day.

It would be a mistake to lead with an image of the food or of your restaurant's front marquee. Instead, we want to tell a story. Maybe it's a story of a couple on their first date, or of another celebrating their anniversary. Either way, we want to sell the idea of intimacy, and how Rose's pasta can provide that through our drink specials. Think about an image of a couple, arm in arm sharing a drink, or of one laughing drink in hand over a candle-lit table. Think about the look a pair of young lovers share when the moment is right. A picture is worth 1,000 words. It's the beat and the melody, and your copy explaining the Valentine's drink deal is the lyrics. If you show Rose's Pasta is a place where the sparks of love ignite and a place where you can get drinks on the cheap, then you've made a hell of a sales pitch to your target audience.

People don't like being sold a product, but they do love being sold a story. So it's your job as a Social Media Manager to tell that story. Storytelling Is one of the oldest human traditions ranging back to the days when we all sat around fires. Invoking the right emotion can speak volumes for the type of brand you are trying to represent. A coffee shop may want to showcase a rainy day and try to invoke a feeling of comfort, while a nightclub may want to aim for a feeling of excitement. Each brand and product will be different in this regard, and the key is to stay true to your brand values and the type of feeling you want your audience to feel when they think about your business.

Chapter 4: Fly The Freak Flag

Let's be honest there is a lot of noise on social media. Whether it's silly cat videos, Memes, or vague postings from our relatives – there's a lot of content that is competing for our attention. So the question becomes how do we stand out?

A common pitfall especially among brands with extremely large budgets is to simply throw money at the problem. More ad spend means more content impressions, and it's an incredibly expensive way to artificially stand out to your audience. For most of us, however, we won't have the luxury of a multi-million dollar ad spend budget. So that means we need to get creative to be more effective.

There are many social media platforms, and it can be daunting to develop and maintain a content strategy on all of them. Is it important to have a presence on most of them? Yes. Is it necessary to spend all your attention to build audiences on all of them? Absolutely not. Let's revisit our customer persona for Rose's Pasta: Swanky Date Spot. David, our 32-year-old tech professional living in Chicago, likely has a presence on multiple social channels but the key is understanding which channel he is the most active on. If your brand is just starting on its Social Marketing journey then you may want to approach it from a multi-channel approach. This will help gauge where your audience is most active, however, if you already have an established audience look to see which channel drives the most engagement. This will give you a better sense of where your audience likes to engage with your brand.

Rose's Pasta, has already dipped their toes in social marketing and knows that their swanky atmosphere, craft cocktails, and gourmet food play well on more visual platforms, like Instagram. Whenever they post on that platform they tend to see much higher levels of likes, comments, and other engagements vs other platforms like Twitter and Facebook. This means their focus should be on Instagram. This is not to say that you can't post from Rose's Pasta on Facebook or Twitter, but it does mean that they should be spending the majority of their ad budget and attention on Instagram. The takeaway here is platform placement can sometimes be more important than what you post. To put it in traditional marketing terms, the right social platform would be akin to publishing a full-page beauty ad for a cosmetic product in a magazine about guns and ammo. Each Platform caters to a different audience and it's up to you to read the data to understand where they are most active. Don't worry, we'll be covering data analytics in a future chapter, to help equip you with the skills to do just that.

In the "standing out equation", platform placement plays a big role, but it's not the only factor to keep in mind. Each Social platform leverages a different algorithm to help prioritize and serve your content to audiences. How these systems work is proprietary information and not publicly available, but I'll share a couple of lessons I had to learn the hard way.

First, you'll want to leverage a multi-media approach. You can't JUST use video, you can't JUST use photos, and you most certainly can't JUST use links. Mixing up your content media type is pivotal to keep your brands positioned as "quality" among the many advertisers across these platforms. This is an unwritten rule, but in my experience a multi-media approach is key. This also gives you an opportunity to think across mediums. How can you convey a Rose's Pasta's Valentine's Day drink special as a Video? As a GIF? As a single photo? Thinking across mediums can help give your creative strategy more legs as you reiterate its execution.

Second, PUBLISH CONSISTENTLY. Consistent publishing schedules are VITAL. If you're a brand that posts twice a week, 30 times the next, and 8 times the week after that, you are NOT publishing consistently. You don't need to publish a million times to get a million conversions. Think about how you can leverage a less is more mentality and focus on quality over quantity. I've found that publishing 3-5 times a week is usually a sweet spot. By having a consistent schedule you will only help rank higher in the algorithm and keep your brand top of mind in your audience's feed.

Third, you'll want to test, test, and test some more! Don't be afraid to break the rules of what is expected. Try different approaches and publishing styles to resonate with your target audience. Don't be so focused on constructing the perfect MLA formatted paragraph, and instead think about how you want your audience to perceive your message. Use all caps, or don't at all. Throw emojis in there and ironic hashtags that have no following. Break the rules of expectation, and let your creative freak flag fly. Many brands have found extreme success by carrying a more playful tone on social than what they'd traditionally use in other marketing mediums. Wendy's i'm looking at you. This isn't to say go right off the rails in the name of science, but don't be afraid to embrace a more creative tone on social even if it is not in line with your 10-page corporate brand guidelines brief.

The beauty of social marketing is that you have measured ways of seeing what works and what doesn't. Be creative and gauge what your audience likes. Figure out what they interact with, and what they don't. Creative ideas stand out, but effective ideas are the ones that resonate with your audience. So let's dive into how we can use the data to help guide us on social execution.

Chapter 5: Let the Numbers Do the Talking

Numbers don't just talk, they shout. They speak the language of success and will be among your strongest indicators of what your next move should be.

Before we dive into a mathematics dissertation, where eyes will gloss over, let's talk about what your goals in Social marketing should be. If you're saying to yourself it's to just sell more, please take a moment and slap yourself for me. When we think about Social Marketing it is far more than "Sales" and "Conversions." Yes, that is a part of the end goal of any marketing campaign, but what makes Social unique is that we can engage in objective-based marketing. This means the goals for our campaigns will differ depending on the objective we are trying to achieve.

If we're looking at objectives from an Ads platform perspective, there are lots of them which range from more engagement, reach, lead generations, and more (each platform offers different objective options). When you leverage these different objectives, each social platform will market your ad differently. For example, if your goal was to get your name out there and enhance brand awareness about a charity that you are sponsoring, the desired result isn't to get a sale or motivate people to your website, but to get eyes on your press or announcement. This is why keeping your objective in mind will help you understand which metric will be your Key Performance Indicator (KPI).

Take a moment and think about a mom-and-pop restaurant you'd like to check out in your hometown. Now think about why it was the first place that came to your mind. Do you pass by it every day on your commute to work? Have you seen fliers for it around town? Maybe a friend mentioned it to you in passing. All of these examples are tied to a business's Brand Awareness; how many people know what your brand is. Some brands are so recognizable you don't even need to see their logo or read their name because it's been engrained so strongly within you. The McDonald's jingle is a prime representation of Brand Awareness. This should highlight why brand awareness objectives can help drive sales, even though they are not directly related. If more people know your brand exists, more people will consider your brand when they are deciding in the future.

For Brand Awareness objectives, there are two KPIs we'll want to look at to help us gauge the effectiveness of our campaigns: Post Impressions, and Post Reach. In terms of industry standards I've seen both used almost interchangeably, but it's important to note the key differences between them to be an effective marketer.

- Post Impressions refer to the total number of people who could see your message. This is important for understanding the depth of potential damage a message may have had during a crisis, or the potential number of people who can or might see your message the next time they open their app. Note: that this does not mean that these people HAVE seen your message, but that they are in the pool of people who could potentially see it. This also means that an individual account can be impressed by your post more than once, the idea being that if a user opens their newsfeed multiple times, there is a potential for your ad to reach them multiple times. Post impressions will ALWAYS be higher than Post reach.

- Post Reach is similar to post impressions, but a bit more exact. Post reach refers to the number of people who HAVE seen your message. However, it's important to understand that seeing a message is not the same as reading it. Have you ever scrolled past an ad on your own newsfeed? Well, that means it's reached you whether you read it or not. This is why standing out with strong visuals and compelling copy is so important to capture your audience's attention. Similar to Post impressions this will account for people who have seen your post multiple times.

For general purposes these will be your two Brand Awareness KPIs, however, there is an argument to be made to look at Unique Post impressions/ Unique Post reach as well. The differences between these are exactly as the name implies. They only account for unique impressions/reach of your post, and will only count individual accounts once, regardless of the number of times a user sees it. This is good information to know, but in my experience, they fail to identify the core metric behind what Brand Awareness seeks to measure. Think back to that hometown restaurant you pass on your way to work; you're not just passing by it once but multiple times a week. Unique impressions/reach fail to account for this. Sometimes it takes 3-8 times of scrolling past an ad for you to actually read it. This is why I would advocate for my customers to use Post Reach/ Impressions instead.

Another Key performance indicator is Engagement, or how many people have liked, commented, shared, or saved your post. This indicates audience interest in a subject, and is a good way to gauge what's effective and what's not. Say you publish two posts for Rose's Pasta, one that speaks to a Happy Hour special, and one that speaks to a dinner special. The one that speaks to Happy Hour ends up receiving 30% more engagements than the dinner special. This tells you that sharing more information about Happy Hour deals is of more interest to your audience. This is why we test, test, and test some more. Say we take that insight and run with it, and publish three more posts that speak to three different drink specials, one for Happy Hour another for the drink of the month, and a third that speaks to our wine selection. We see that both the wine selection and drink of the month flop in terms of engagement. What does this tell you? Your audience is not just interested in knowing more about drinks but Happy Hour specials specifically. Continue testing iterations on this. Would the audience care more about wine-specific Happy Hour specials? What about Happy Hour food specials? Was it the image of the cocktail on the original ad that they engaged with over the messaging of the drink special? These are all questions you can test, and through engagement have a concrete number to help guide you to insights about your target audience.

Similar to Engagement, another KPI to measure is Link Clicks. After all in most cases, you'll want to leverage your CTA to drive your audiences to click a link to complete a marketed action. Again, sales shouldn't be the only key indicator you're solving for, but at the end of the day, that's what's going to get you paid. Link Clicks refers to the number of people who click the link you share. It's always important to check Link Clicks independently of engagement because in most cases people who click your link will be driven off the social network and fail to engage with your post. To say, engagement is a way to gauge audience interest in your campaign, while a link click is the number of people who are partaking in the desired action you want to drive to. In some cases, you'll find that the extremely low-engaged content post is your top performer in terms of link clicks, and a highly engaged piece of content is among your lowest drivers of clicks. High-engaged content keeps you ranked higher in the algorithm over time, but high-click content means you're having a more favorable effect. This is why both metrics are important for the continued success of your brand and should be optimized and measured separately.

Have a testing mindset and never be daunted by poor social marketing performance. Everything is a lesson you can use to enhance the next campaign. Say you share a post for every food item you have on the Rose's Pasta menu, and all of them flop. That's an indicator that your audience doesn't want to see your food, and maybe they are more interested in something else – like ambiance, drinks, or service quality. Maybe it's an indicator of the quality of messaging and imagery you're using. Either way, there is a lesson to be learned from any campaign whether it goes viral or flops. The key is to never be discouraged and to fail quickly, learn, and reiterate.

I'd love to sit here and say boom, it's just as easy as looking at engagement and you can call it a day and go home, but you'll see especially the more you work with social data things are rarely ever that clear-cut. Post reach/Impressions work in concert with engagements. Let's say you have a post that has a post reach of 1,000 people and has 90 total engagements (defined as likes, comments, and shares) and another post that has reached 100 people and has a total of 50 engagements. Which post had the higher performance? If you guessed the first post you're wrong. The industry standard metric to standardize the variance in performance across posts is called the Engagement rate. Don't worry the calculation for this is as easy as Total Engagement – Total Post Reach. With this in mind, the first post would have an engagement rate of .09%, while the second post would have an engagement rate of 50%. A 50% engagement rate is ridiculously high, but illustrates my point. In most cases, a good engagement rate will range from 1-3%. Anything above that means you've found gold and a highly engaged campaign concept.

Now it's time for some hard truths, especially if you're like me and consider yourself more of the creative type. A creative mentality will take you far in an ad agency brainstorming session, but won't carry much water when it comes to gauging social performance. Let the numbers do the talking. Sometimes insanely creative ideas flop because it wasn't what the audience wanted, and conversely sometimes boring creative drives massive success for a campaign. Creative ideas will help you stand out but don't bet the house on it because you have become married to the concept. If your audience likes a more buttoned-up and traditional approach to advertising, then button up your creative and speak to them the way they want to be spoken to. Not every brand gets to be Wendy's, and not every brand has to speak like Mercedes Benz. Finding your brand's voice on social may take time, testing, and patience to find the right fit. Let the data guide you to what's right for your brand.

Conclusion

As you may have realized there is no one-size-fits-all approach to Social Marketing. Each brand, service, and product will have nuanced that is determined by who you are advertising to and the type of marketing objective you want to achieve.

Through testing and learning more about your audience, you can find the path forward. You can iterate and reiterate creative concepts to help find your identity and get you started on how to speak to your audiences. So really the next step is to get out there and see what works.

I hope this book has helped set a foundation of what areas you should focus on to help optimize your marketing strategies and to inspire you to stand out and try something new. Social marketing can be an incredibly fun way for your brand to interact with your audience while also teaching you more about what they crave.

But if you take nothing else from this book take these 5 lessons:

- Know your audience.
- Less is more when it comes to social copy.
- Sell a story.
- Don't be afraid to stand out.

- Test, test, and test some more.

If you keep these lessons in the back of your mind, you will without a doubt achieve marketing success on Social.

9 7 9 8 8 7 6 1 6 8 0 6 1